15+

D0784331

First published in 2008
by Franklin Watts

Franklin Watts
338 Euston Road
London NW1 3BH

Franklin Watts Australia
Level 17/207 Kent Street
Sydney, NSW 2000

A CIP catalogue record for this book
is available from the British Library.

ISBN: 978 0 7496 7717 6

Printed in Great Britain

Franklin Watts is a division of Hachette Children's Books,
an Hachette Livre UK company.
www.hachettelivre.co.uk

Speed Freaks

Spike T. Adams

Illustrated by John Charlesworth

W
FRANKLIN WATTS
LONDON•SYDNEY

Chapter 1

Marlon and me are winning.

Biggest street race this city has ever seen.

From one side to the other.

I can almost feel the prize money in my hand.

Taste the glory in my mouth.

"What's happening, Dex?" Marlon asks.

He keeps his eyes on the road ahead.

I scan the radio. No police.

"All clear!" I say.

I don't see the van.

Cuts us up out of nowhere.

Marlon has to brake. Hard.

One car goes past. Then two others.

Three more.

"You shouda seen that coming!" Marlon shouts at me.

He puts his foot down.

Slams his fist on the steering wheel.

"We'll never catch them now!"

He's well vexed. I've let him down.

Too busy thinking about the money.

I have to come up with something.

Fast!

And then I see we are near The Cut.

"Look!" I say. "If we take The Cut we can make up time."

I wait for Marlon to thank me.

But he just shakes his head. "No way, man," he snaps.

"Why not?" I ask.

"I heard that place is jinxed," Marlon tells me.

I stare at him.

Think of the money.

"It's The Cut or we lose!" I yell.

Marlon's hands grip the wheel.

"OK. Let's do it," he says.

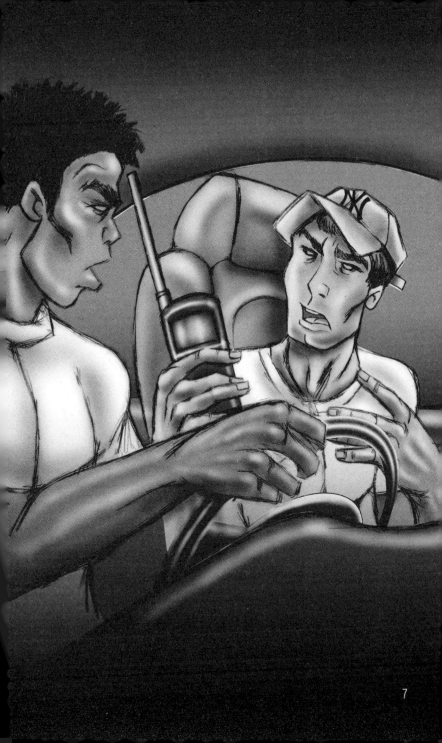

Chapter 2

The Cut is too dark, too narrow.

The air feels colder.

The radio crackles.

There are voices.

New voices.

I can't make out what they're saying.

We drive on into the gloom.

The car headlights flicker.

"This is weird, man!" I say.

"We can't turn back now!" Marlon says.

He presses the pedal.

"We just gotta keep on going!"

And then she walks out in front of us.

A girl.

"Marlon! Stop!" I yell.

Marlon hits the brakes.

But nothing happens.

The girl looks right at us.

She screams.

And then CRACK!

She hits the bonnet.

Bounces over the car.

Falls away on to the road.

We keep going - out of control.

Another body hits the car.

Bounces off it.

Then another.

Another. ANOTHER.

And then suddenly we are out of The Cut.

The car begins to slow down.

"The brakes work again," says Marlon.

We skid sideways and stop.

We sit there. In shock.

"Shit..." Marlon whispers.

I can't speak.

I just stare out of the window.

Outside, it looks like we're still moving.

The buildings are all blurred.

Like we are driving past them.

But we're not.

What is this place?

13

Chapter 3

Up ahead I see some people.

"Let's ask for help," I say, opening the car door.

Marlon nods.

The air outside is thick with traffic fumes.

I can taste them.

They burn the back of my throat.

The moving buildings make me dizzy.

I try not to look at them.

"This is way too weird, man..." Marlon says.

I nod. "Come on," I say.

I just want out of here.

We start walking.

We get closer.

The people are all mashed up.

Bodies all twisted.

Skin ripped and bleeding.

"The car came out of nowhere..." a girl sobs.

"He just ran me down!"

Blood and tears seep from her eyes.

"He just kept on driving!" says another.

"I don't think they're gonna help us," I say to Marlon.

We begin to turn back.

But there are more of them behind us.

Blocking our way.

Getting closer.

"What the hell are these?" Marlon hisses.

"I dunno!" I say.

A little girl limps forward.

She's dragging a dead dog.

She looks up at us with one white eye.

"Too fast!" she cries.

My heart is thumping in my chest.

I can hardly breathe.

"Run!" Marlon shouts.

We run.

Chapter 4

We race down the street.

They follow us.

The whole place is wrong and warped.

Left feels like right. Up feels like down.

There are more of them on every corner.

Everywhere we turn.

And then we hit a dead end.

We back up against the wall.

Nowhere to go.

"Shit. We're going to die," says Marlon.

The mob gets closer.

Muttering and moaning all the time.

So close, I can smell their rotting flesh.

My heart feels like it's gonna stop.

Then I hear the growl of an engine.

A car bombs up the street.

Headlights blazing.

It brakes and skids round in front of us.

From inside, a voice yells, "Get in!"

We don't need telling twice.

Chapter 5

The driver is Aaron.

I remember him.

He's a street racer — he went missing.

A girl comes up to the car.

She bangs on the glass.

"Why?" she asks him.

"Shut up!" Aaron screams at her. "Leave me alone!"

The girl shakes her head.

Now I see the other side of her face.

It's hanging off.

Aaron canes it back down the street.

Smashes into the girl.

Crashes through the rest of the mob.

"Where the hell are we?" Marlon shouts.

"Welcome to The Zone, my friends," says Aaron.

"You took The Cut, didn't you?" he asks.

"Yeah," we say.

"Bad move," he tells us.

"It's a trap. Brings you
to this place. To them."

"Who are they?" I ask.

"I call them Zone Freaks. Killed by speeding drivers. They want their revenge. So they hang out at The Zone to torment their killers."

"How did you end up here?" I ask Aaron.

"Same as you," he says. "Took The Cut to win a race."

Marlon looks at me, like this is all my fault.

"That girl..." I say to Aaron. "She seemed to know you..."

Aaron slows down a little.

"She stepped out in front of me in a race," he says.

"I'd have lost if I'd stopped."

He turns to look at us. "You both know how it is. It's all about winning, right?"

My mouth is dry. I can't speak.

"Whatever..." Marlon says. "Look, we got in here
— so there must be a way out!"

Aaron laughs.

The hollow sound of it makes me shudder.

"Oh, yes," he agrees. "There is a way to get out."

"Well? Tell us then!" Marlon says.

Aaron looks at us both. "You race for it. Rules are
simple. One lap of the ring road. Winner gets to
leave."

He slows down.

I look out and see we're back at our car.

There's someone sitting on the bonnet.

"I've been waiting for someone to race," Aaron says.

I swallow, hard. "What happens to the loser?" I ask him.

Aaron laughs again. "Loser stays."

Chapter 6

We make a run for the car.

On the bonnet. It's the girl we ran down
in The Cut.

The mob rushes from round a corner.

Moaning and crying.

They're gonna block us off.

I hear Aaron fire up his engine.

He blares out his horn — drives into them.

A path clears for us.

"Go!" I shout at Marlon.

We sprint through the gap.

Push the girl out of the way.

Yank the car doors open.

Slam them shut just in time.

Outside the Zone Freaks gather again.

All around the car.

We need to get going and fast.

"Aaron's been in this place for ages," I say.

"He'll know all the shortcuts."

Marlon revs the engine.

"Then we need to stick close to him."

He stabs the car into first gear.

"Pick the right moment. We'll only get one chance," he says.

I nod.

Now we race.

We rip through the bodies.

Into the smoke and stink of The Zone.

We're alongside Aaron's car.

We slam into each other.

Metal screeches against metal.

Sparks fly.

Marlon is caning it. Tyres squealing as we dodge smashed-up cars.

The Zone Freaks watch us on every street.

They're all chanting one word.

Over and over again.

"Crash. Crash. Crash. Crash."

Then I spot something up ahead.

Part of the road — it's blocked!

Looks like a row of broken down cars.

There's only enough room for one car to pass.

"Move right! Move right!" I shout.

We grind up against Aaron's car again.

We've got more power.

We get there just before him.

He follows us.

"We've got him now!" I shout.

"Yeah, he'll never catch up," says Marlon.

"We're going home. Woo hoo!"

Chapter 7

There's a bridge up ahead.

It's loaded with Zone Freaks.

Hundreds of them.

As we go under it, they jump.

A rain of screaming monsters.

THUD!

Hitting the bonnet.

BANG!

Hanging onto the sides.

To slow us down.

To keep us here.

45

"Get them off!" I scream.

Something grabs my head.

I look up.

The sun roof. It's open!

A Zone Freak is reaching in.

Her nails hack at my face.

I grab her head. Push her back.

Her face is slick with blood and tears and snot.

And my thumb slides into her eye.

It collapses into her head.

"Errggg!"

47

Marlon swerves hard.

The force of it pushes the Freak off the car.

She falls back onto the road.

"You OK?" Marlon shouts.

"Just about!" I shout back.

I press the button to close the sun roof.

I almost do it.

But then another Freak pokes its head in.

He reaches out an arm.

"They just ran me down..." he sobs. "WHY?"

"Get rid of it!" Marlon screams.

I keep my finger on the button.

The hand keeps trying to grab me.

I grit my teeth. The sun roof closes.

Something heavy falls on my leg.

It's the Freak's arm.

All I can do is stare at it.

The fingers start to move.

I yell and scoop it up.

It lands on Marlon. Grabs his nuts.

"Shit! Shit! Shit!" he shouts.

"Get it off me!"

I shake my head. I can't touch it again.

Marlon takes a hand off the wheel.

Slows down while he chucks the arm onto the back seat.

Aaron's car sweeps past us.

Chapter 8

Up ahead Aaron's car completes the lap.

It vanishes.

All that's left is the smoke from his exhaust.

This can't be it.

"Follow him!" I shout at Marlon.

Marlon shakes his head.

"You heard what Aaron said. Only the winners get out."

The car splutters.

Stops dead.

"OK then. We just have to keep on driving, like Aaron did," I say.

Marlon grunts. "Then what?" he asks.

"When someone else gets here, we race!" I say.

"And next time, we'll win."

Marlon looks down at the dashboard.

"There's just one problem with that plan, Dex," he says.

The monsters close in on us.

Moaning. Shuffling.

Marlon points to the fuel gauge.

The needle points to empty.

"Oh Shit!"

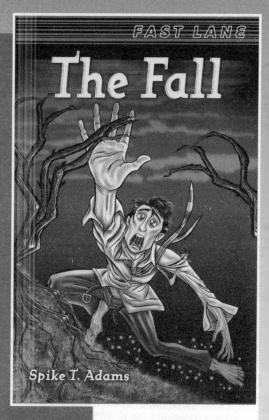

978 0 7496 7718 3

Jon feels bad about Ricky.

Ricky's a geek. A loser.

He gets picked on all the time.

But never hits back.

Then one day, up at the Outlook, Ricky is pushed way too far...

FAST LANE

The Hide

Spike T. Adams

978 0 7496 7719 0

Jase is on the run.

Dale and his crew are gonna mash him up.

So Tasha takes Jase inside the Hide.

Where he finds out her bloody secret…

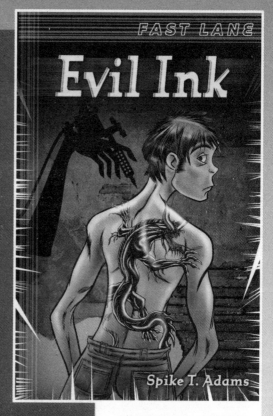

978 0 7496 7716 9

Tom is getting no respect.

So he gets a killer tattoo.

The demon on Tom's back does the job.

It brings him respect.

But it also brings something far more terrible...